Love dreaming & other poems

Ali Cobby Eckermann

Love dreaming
& other poems

Vagabond Press | Indigenous Australian Writing

Published by Vagabond Press.
PO Box 958 Newtown NSW 2042 Australia
www.vagabondpress.net
First edition published in 2012.
Transnational edition published in 2014.

© Ali Cobby Eckermann 2012, 2014.
Cover image © Kay Orchison, excerpt from *Trajectories VI/I,* 2008-2012.

Designed and typeset by Michael Brennan
in Minion Pro 11/14.5

All rights reserved. No part of this publication may be reproduced, stored in a retrieval system or transmitted in any form or by any means electronic, mechanical, photocopying or otherwise without the prior permission of the publisher. The information and views set out in this book are those of the author(s) and do not necessarily reflect the opinion of the publisher.

ISBN 978-1-922181-72-5

This book is
for my walytja

Minya Audrey, Jonnie and Tamia
Shakaya, Rivah and Syaura

Acknowledgments: *Antipodes, Being Human* (Bloodaxe Books, 2011), *Best Australian Poems 2009* (Black Inc, 2009), *Best Australian Poems 2010* (Black Inc, 2010), *Fish Tails in the Dust* (Ptilotus Press, 2009), *Kami* (Vagabond Press, 2011), *Little Bit Long Time* (Australian Poetry Centre, 2009; Picaro Press, 2010), *Indigenous Etchings Treaty* (Ilura Press, 2011), *My Country Anytime Anywhere* (IAD Press, 2010), *Poezica Magazine.*

CONTENTS

Kami 9
Grade One Primary 10
Wildflowers 11
That Summer Before The War 12
Dingo Eye 13
Mai 14
Shells 15
Sink 16
Resurrection 17
Tears For Mum 18
Love Dreaming 19
First Time 20
The Mountain 21
Kumana 22
2 Pelicans 23
Faiku 25
Killing Fields 26
Shrine 27
Ribbons 28
Table Manners 29
Little Bit Long Time 30
I Tell You True 31
1 Child 2 Child 33
Town Camp 34
Emptiness 35
How Does A Father Feel? 36
Message 37

Circles & Squares 38
Ngankari 40
Sunrise 41
Intervention Allies 42
40-Year Leases 43
A Parable 44
Intervention Pay Back 45
Palya 50
True Love 51
Black 52
Yabun 53
Anangu Love Poems 54
Tjamu 56
Wallaroo 57

Notes 60

KAMI

I walk to the south
I walk to the north
Where are you
My Warrior

I sit with the desert
I sit with the ocean
Where are you
My Warrior

I sing in the sand
I sing with the rocks
Where are you
My Warrior

I dance with the birds
I dance with the animals
Where are you
My Warrior

Heaven is everywhere
Where are you

GRADE ONE PRIMARY

I'm sitting up the tree today
And I'm NOT getting down!
I don't feel safe at school no more
Just 'cos my skin is brown.
If I sit here overnight
Will I turn into a bird?
So I can fly away from here
And all the nasty words

'Cos it's no fun being different
Where do I fit in?
Some kids at school are nasty
And their words have such a sting.
You half-caste dog, you coon, you boong,
You stinking bloody abo,
I don't know what these words mean –
I know they hurt me like an arrow.

I asked my teacher to explain
And she just slapped me hard
And then when it was lunchtime
I was pushed over in the yard.
So now I'm sitting up the tree
I'll hide from everyone.
I don't understand this place –
I'm only in Grade One.

WILDFLOWERS

Mallets pound fence posts
in tune with the sabres
to mask massacre sites

Cattle will graze
sheep hooves will scatter
children's bones

Wildflowers won't grow
where bone powder
lies

THAT SUMMER BEFORE THE WAR

I saw you
dance
your face painted
proudly celebrates
your hunting skills

the headdress
reflects
your rightful place
of leadership
and wisdom

women in awe
whisper
behind their hands
of your strength
and bravery

that was
before
the white man
came and
killed you

DINGO EYE

Serpentine Gorge is empty
shiny heat wave shimmer
birds have flown the billabong

frogs bury, dormant for rain
I peer into eyes of dingo
airless, motionless

we hold that stare
before breath expires
before understanding

a blink of my eye
the dingo vanishes
with fading dusk

MAI

Early morning mist
Periwinkles
Ocean spray off Nullabor cliffs

Dunes of white sand
Lizards
Spinifex land

Open skies
Fish
The far hint of rain

Afternoon tree shade
Wild figs
Camp at Clara Bay

Footprints don't fade
Culture
Kami May

SHELLS

in an aisle
of middens
he blocks her
advance

they laugh
as they prepare
for war
his shiny shell

embellished spear
in hand
watching her
body paint

in white ochre
her breasts
her stomach
her thighs

glisten white
on alabaster
skin soon
to turn red

SINK

every time we argue
I grieve the loss of you
you are leaving
there will be no farewell kiss at the door
you are returning to your country

and probably your ex-wife
or the wife before that
or the wife before her (sic)
your children will tell you things
they didn't like me
I wasn't good enough for you
I was …

at the sink he says
gee he says *you stolen generation mob*
you're really affected!
we was only arguing
whose turn to do the dishes!

RESURRECTION

my teenage Spirit
has grown old
hold the knife
slash the world
      away
your black hand
holds mine bleached
by Christianity
bleached to fit in to
      survive
I hope you rise
like Jesus
but not where
I can see you
      yet

TEARS FOR MUM

Mum can I cry at your funeral, can I wail
Like I do out bush, can I walk the aisle in ochre
Can you tell the other kids that this is okay, this is
What I need, the way we grieve, proper way out bush

Mum can you explain that I need my sisters from Yuendumu
And Haasts Bluff by my side at your funeral
Can you tell the other kids that this is okay, this is
What I need, the way we grieve, proper way out bush

Mum can you understand this is the only way I know
To mend my aching heart when you pass away
Can you tell the other kids that this is okay, this is
What I need, the way we grieve, proper way out bush

LOVE DREAMING

When you went back to the waterhole
and sat under the mulberry tree
at the Ooldea soakage
Did you see Daisy Bates
dressed in English attire
standing on the white sand dunes?

When you went back to the waterhole
and scooped the precious water
from the sandy sanctuary
Did you hear the warriors
dancing in the moonlight
Snake and Emu making love?

When you went to the waterhole
Do the white sand dunes
Make love to the moonlight?
Does the mulberry tree
Scoop the precious water?
Does Daisy hear the warriors
Coming back, coming back.

FIRST TIME (I MET MY GRANDMOTHER)

Sit down in the dirt and brush away the flies
Sit down in the dirt and notice the many eyes

I never done no wrong to you, so why you look at me?
But if you gotta check me out, well go ahead – feel free!

I feel that magic thing you do, you crawl beneath my skin
To read the story of my Soul, well I'm telling you I'm clean

And now yous' mob won't talk to me, so I just sit and sit
English words seem useless, I know Language just a bit

I sit alone, not lonely, 'cos this country sings loud Songs
I've never even been here before, but I feel like I belong

It's three days, here come the mob, big smiles are on their face
"This your grandmother's Country here, this is your homeland place"

"We got a shock when we seen you, you got your Nana's face
We was real sad when she went missing in that cold Port pirie place"

I understand my feelings now, tears push behind my eyes
I'll sit on this soil anytime, and brush away them flies

I'll dance with mob on this red land, munda wiru place
I'll dance away those half caste lies, 'cos I got my Nana's face.

THE MOUNTAIN

my lips are cracked and bleeding
my Language lies
dried up on my tongue

my hands have grown blisters
the skills of my Ancestors
are clumsy on my fingers

yet my eyes still shine

the mountain is watching me
always dragging my eyes back
around to grasp its view

what is it showing me?
what will I learn?

I sit

and

I watch

and

I wait

KUMANA

There is no life
but Family.

When I am young
I live with my Family.

When I grow up
I leave my Family.

When I am lonely
I miss my Family.

When I am drunk
I reverse-charge my Family.

When I pass away
I unite my Family.

There is no life
but Family.

2 PELICANS

My friend was at the hospital, he wasn't feeling good
I was at the barbecue, just like he said I should.
The phone call from the hospital shocks me with fear and fright
"You better come to ICU, he might not make it through the night."

I stand silent at his bedside, he looks so dead already,
I try comforting his children as their lives become unsteady.
"Please don't go away," I whisper, "Don't leave them behind."
I pray then to my Ancestors, I ask them for a sign.

We sit all night like statues, on each side of his bed,
The thought of losing him is really fucking with my head!
The nursing staff fuss round with looks of deep regret.
But I was waiting for a sign that he won't leave us yet.

The morning light creeps slowly across red desert sand
His eyelids flicker open and he fumbles for my hand.
"Hello" he whispers "how are you?" and then falls back to sleep
My eyes stare at the monitors, the bips, the dots, the beeps.

"He's out of danger," the doctor says, "you should get some rest"
And as I walked along Gap Road I look out to the west
2 pelicans fly overhead, floating on the breeze,
"It's the sign," I cry and thank the Spirits watching over me.

I return to the hospital, he is much stronger now
And the nursing staff all smiling as they too wonder how?
I share the story of the sign, the pelicans in the sky
We hold each others hands and smiles are in our eyes.

I drive out to Amoonguna to tell family he is right
I sit down with his Aunty, round the campfire, in the night
I ask her to explain the pelicans and the meaning of the sign
She laughs and whispers "Arrangkwe just 2 pelicans in the sky!"

FAIKU

I drink in the street
ask for money each day
intolerance is free

when I pass away
alone under the bridge
weeds grow in your mouth

a paupers grave
dead flowers bent backward
broken by neglect

KILLING FIELDS

did they kill 'em here?
I ask the guide
quietly staring
into the distance
over the bay.
*why? do you
feel something?*
she asks with
trepidation.
nah! I say
*it's just that
they got killed
every other place
I been to.
not here*
she smiles
with pride.

SHRINE

Among the rubble
I reconstruct a roof
From battered rusty tin
Sunlight sparkles through
Old nail holes
As will stars and droplets
Of refreshing rain

Every stone I hold
In my gaze
In my hands
Wait for its voice
Wait for its destination
Wait to embalm with muddy earth

I build large windows
And gaze in awe where
Clouded glass sits
No longer

I sweep the earthen
Floor with tenderness
Remove impurities
From its skin
As it has done
Mine.

RIBBONS

"See you," I said to the children
as I memorised
their Anangu faces
filled with laughter
and trust for family
innocent in their youth
and strong in culture

"See you," I said to the Elders
as the tears flow
in my heart
and I bend down
to shake their hands
and gain my strength
by skin

"See you," I said at Maralinga
and the dust from my car
as I drove away
was like a ribbon
across the desert sand
tying me to that place
forever

TABLE MANNERS

Warrior woman walks proudly
Close to where I sit in the street.
I notice her muted smile buried behind her scars.
Our eyes meet.

I bow my head.
"Sorry sis," I say quietly, "I got nothing."
My friend looks at me, searches through her bag,
"I might have something?"

I respect the warrior woman, ask, "What's your name?"
Her eyes are focused behind me.
Focused on another place
Along Todd Mall.

Suddenly her focus is at my shoulder,
"We told you before," waitress **yells** in my ear.
"You have to leave."
"You can't ask for money here."

Warrior woman walks proudly
Away from where I sit today.
Her scarred face turns, smiles with her words – "She's just jealous!"

LITTLE BIT LONG TIME

"Stay here,"
he whispers gruffly   holds her roughly
hugs her   then hides her
little bit long time

Big eyes young face   stare from hiding place
watch her Dad pause   check nature's laws
sniffing the air   eyes filled with despair
little bit long time

He just wants some water   to give to his daughter
he steps from the trees   crawls on his knees
squats in the sand   drinks with his hands
little bit long time

Her eyes do not waver   good lessons he gave her
sees Dad fall over strange   there a hole in his brains
gun noise fills her ears   her eyes lose their tears
little bit long time

Rough white hands snatch her   cruel voices scratch her
she's too scared to run   she's learnt respect for the gun
two different eyes clash   she knows in a flash
this killer had watched them

little bit long time

I TELL YOU TRUE

I can't stop drinking, I tell you true
Since I watched my daughter perish
She burned to death inside a car
I lost what I most cherish
I saw the angels hold her
As I screamed with useless hope
I can't stop drinking, I tell you true
It's the only way I cope!

I can't stop drinking, I tell you true
Since I found my sister dead
She hung herself to stop the rapes
I found her in the shed
The rapist bastard still lives here
Unpunished in this town
I can't stop drinking, I tell you true
Since I cut her down

I can't stop drinking, I tell you true
Since my mother passed away
They found her battered down the creek
I miss her more each day
My family blamed me for her death
Their words have made me wild
I can't stop drinking, I tell you true
'Cos I was just a child.

So if you see someone like me
Who's drunk and loud and cursing
Don't judge too hard, you never know
What sorrows we are nursing.

1 CHILD 2 CHILD WAILING AND WILD

Urgent darkness hunts us south, while my stomach churns
    with childbirth
He waits.

Foetal juices of Blood and Life baptise this child from my womb
He waits.

I wash my child with sand of red, avoid newborn eyes of Trust,
    with Love
He waits.

A feeble cry escapes the grave. I watch it enter Heaven
He waits.

Red Band, Black Man, Husband and Father, gently holds our
    toddler daughter
He has watched mine; now I watch his back, survival dictates
    our nomadic trek

We walk silent strong in single file fashion, stumble our way
    to the mission
He waits.

I bite and kick and scratch and scream "Don't take this child
    from me!"
He waits.
I sit broken beside him. The darkness is no longer urgent.

TOWN CAMP

You call it 3 bedroom house
I call him big lotta trouble

You call it electricity
I call him too much tv

You call it litter
I call him progress

You call it graffiti
I call him reading and writing

You call it vandalism
I call him payback

You call it a sad urban environment
I call him home

EMPTINESS

the big black bird struts proudly
    defiantly
along my front fence garden
"Faark" it screeches loudly

the whole street can hear
yet no movement
no one walking around
no friendship
no sense of community

a knock at the window
and I look out quickly
a branch bangs on the glass again
the breeze blows by
an empty beer can rattles
rolls along the empty street

the big black bird struts proudly
    defiantly
along my front fence garden
"Faark" it screeches loudly

I sit inside thinking
exactly the same thing

HOW DOES A FATHER FEEL?

How does a father feel
After his child is abused?

Does he want to kill the man
Who stole innocence forever?
Does he want to sit alone
And hide, pretend, whatever?

Does he want to hit his wife
When her crying goes on and on?

Does he want to go drinking
With his mates, even that one?

What does a father feel
After his child is abused?

Kill hide hit deny
Speak to that man, even that one.

MESSAGE

Every grain of sand in this
big red country
is a pore on the skin
of my Family

Every feather on the ground in this
spinifex country
is a spiritual message
from my Ancestors.

Every wild flower that blooms in this
desert of red
is a signpost of hope
for my People.

CIRCLES AND SQUARES

I was born Yankunytjatjara
My Mother is Yankunytjatjara
Her Mother was Yankunytjatjara
My Family is Yankunytjatjara

I have learnt many things from my Family Elders
I have grown to recognise that my Life travels in Circles
My Aboriginal Culture has taught me that
Universal Life is Circular

When I was born I was not allowed to live with my Family
I grew up in the white man's world

We lived in a Square house
We picked fruit and vegetables from a neatly fenced Square plot
We kept animals in Square paddocks
We sat and ate at a Square table
We sat on Square chairs
I slept in a Square bed

I looked at myself in a Square mirror and did not know who I was

One day I met my Mother
I just knew that this meeting was part of our Healing Circle
Then I began to travel
I visited places that I had been before

But this time I sat down with Family
We gathered closely Together by big Round campfires
We ate bush tucker, feasting on Round ants and berries
We ate meat from animals that lived in Round burrows
We slept in Circles on beaches around Our fires
We sat in the dirt, on Our Land, that belongs to a big Round planet
        We watched the Moon grow to a magnificent yellow Circle

That was Our Time

I have learnt two different ways now
I am thankful for this
That is part of my Life Circle

My heart is Round like a drum, ready to echo the music of my Family

But the Square within me still remains
The Square hole stops me in my entirety.

NGANKARI

arms wrap round Kami
smell the campfire hair
Seven Sisters dancing
Pleiades all night
chanting and singing
laughing and joy
in the morning
big clean-up time
women scramble in
Toyota dreaming
dust trails linger
the girl waits
signal from the ochre man
ngankari ngankari
sickness is gone
you good now girl
go get the world

SUNRISE

I see you Kami
more beautiful
than a sunrise
at Pipalyatjara
wind swept
red inma clouds
watching over

I hear you Kami
telling stories
at Coober Pedy
old wisdoms
standing on sand dunes
watching over
Kupa Piti Kungka Tjuta

Franky Yamma sings
talk this way   walk this way
wangka anyinyi   tjina anyinyi
guide my journey back
through the mix up mayhem

I feel you Kami
sitting on the munda
wailing away another
half caste day

INTERVENTION ALLIES

When john howard said
let's have an intervention
the women shouted yes!
we're sick of the drinking
the weekend footy trips away
happy hours in hotels
without bringing their pay home to us
and sometimes losing their jobs
when they don't know when to stop
we're sick of the sarcasm
the fights the occasional black eye
their priority for their mates
over us and the children
we're sick of their drunken breath
exploding in unjustified abuse
the words that can't be retrieved
when he crawls back into bed
Yes the women shouted
let's have the intervention

The Aboriginal women
weren't so sure.

40-YEAR LEASES

high on compensation
they tell me right from wrong
say the old days are over
you gotta sign the paper
coming on the charter plane
all friendly sitting round
say we gonna fix this place
you gotta sign the paper
I sign the paper
charter planes fly away
no more sit down circle
I wait for the fixing
my wife says
what you waiting for
come fishing with us
just like the old days

A PARABLE

Interventionists are coming, interventionists are coming
the cries echo throughout the dusty community
as the army arrive in their chariots
parents and children race for the sandhills
burying the tommy axes and the *rifela*
hiding in abandoned cars along the fence line

One woman ran to the waterhole
hiding her baby in the reeds
dusting her footprints with gumleaf
other children went and got their cousin
shouting "mum you gone rama rama
you should see the clinic."

That night the woman went back to the waterhole
leaving her child in the reeds again this time in a basket.
in the morning the children return holding their cousin
crying "mum you gone rama rama
    you should see the doctor."

At the clinic I feel her pulse check
her blood pressure test for diabetes
staring deeply in my eyes
until finally our heads bent
she whispers quietly in Luritja
"this son name is Moses."

INTERVENTION PAY BACK

I love my wife   she right skin for me   pretty one my
wife   young one   found her at the next community over
across the hills   little bit long way   not far

and from there she give me good kids   funny kids mine
we always laughing
all together   and that wife   she real good mother   make
our wali real nice   flowers and grass patch and chickens
I like staying home with my kids

and from there I build cubby house   yard for the horse
see I make them things from left overs   from the dump
all the left overs from fixing the houses
and all the left overs I build cubby house and chicken house

and in the house we teach the kids   don't make mess   go
to school learn good so you can work round here later
good job   good life   and the government will leave you alone

and from there tjamu and nana tell them the story   when
the government was worse   rations   government make up
all the rules   but don't know culture   can't sit in the sand
oh tjamu and nana   they got the best story   we always
laughing us mob

and from there night time when we all asleep   all together
on the grass patch   dog and cat and kids   my wife and
me   them kids they ask really good questions about the

olden days   about today   them real ninti them kids
they gunna be right

and from there come intervention   John Howard   he
make new rules   he never even come to see us   how good
we was doing already   Mal Brough   he come with the
army   we got real frightened true   thought he was gonna
take the kids away   just like tjamu and nana bin tell us

I run my kids in the sand hills   took my rifle up there and
sat   but they was all just lying   changing their words all
the time   wanting meeting today and meeting tomorrow
we was getting sick of looking at them   so everyone put
their eyes down   and some even shut their ears

and from there I didn't care too much   just kept working
fixing the housing   being happy working hard   kids go
to school   wife working hard too   didn't care too much
we was right   we always laughing us mob   all together

but then my wife she come home crying   says the money
in quarantine but I didn't know why they do that   we
was happy   not drinking and fighting   why they do that
we ask the council   t*o stop the drinking and protect the
children*   hey you know me ya bloody mongrel I don't
drink   and I look after my kids   I bloody fight ya you
say that again   *hey settle down   we not saying that   Mal
Brough saying that   don't you watch the television   he
making the rules for all the mobs   every place Northern
Territory   he real cheeky whitefella   but he's the boss we
gotta do it*

and from there I tell my wife she gets paid half   half in
hand half in the store   her money in the store now   half
and half   me too   all us building mob   but I can't buy
tobacco   or work boots   you only get the meat and bread
just like the mission days   just like tjamu and nana tell us

and from there I went to the store to get meat for our
supper   but the store run out   only tin food left   so I
asked for some bullets   I'll go shoot my own meat   but
sorry they said   you gotta buy food   that night I slept
hungry   and I slept by myself
thinking about it

and from there the government told us our job was finish
the government bin give us the sack   we couldn't believe
it   we been working CDEP for years   slow way we park
the truck at the shed   just waiting   for something   for
someone with tobacco

the other men's reckon   fuck this   drive to town for the
grog   but I stayed with my kids   started watching the
television   trying to laugh   not to worry   just to be like
yesterday

and from there   the politician man says *I give you real
job*   tells me to work again   but different   only half time
sixteen hours but I couldn't understand   it was the same job
as before   but more little   less pay   and my kids can't
understand   when they come home from school   why I
cant buy the lolly for them   like I used to before   I didn't
want to tell them   I get less money for us now

and from there they say my wife earns too much money   I
gonna miss out again   I'm getting sick of it   don't worry
she says   I'll look after you   but I know that's not right
way   I'm getting shame   my brother   he shame too   he
goes to town drinking   leaves his wife behind   leaves his
kids

and from there I drive round to see tjamu   he says his
money in the store too   poor bloke   he can't even walk
that far   and I don't smile   I look at the old man   he lost
his smile too   but nana she cook the damper and roo tail
she trying to smile   she always like that

and from there when I get home   my wife gone to town
with the sister in law   she gone look for my brother   he
might be stupid on the grog   he not used to it   she gotta
find him   might catch him with another woman   make
him bleed   drag him home

and from there my wife   she come back   real quiet   tells
me she went to casino   them others took her   taught
her the machines   she lost all the money   she lost her
laughing

and from there all the kids bin watching us   quiet way
not laughing around   so we all go swimming down the
creek   all the families there together   we happy again
them boys   we take them shooting   chasing the malu in
the car   we real careful with the gun   not gonna hurt my
kids no way

and from there my wife   she sorry   she back working
hard   save the money   kids gonna get new clothes   I
gonna get my tobacco and them bullets   but she gone
change again   getting her pay   forgetting her family
forget yesterday   only thinking for town   with the sister
in law

and my wife   she got real smart now   drive for miles all
dressed up   going to the casino with them other kungkas
for the Wednesday night draw

I ready told you I love my kids   I only got five   two pass
away already   and I not complaining bout looking after
my kids   no way   but when my wife gets home   if she
spent all the money   not gonna share with me and the kids

I might hit her   first time

PALYA

palya he say
in cultural way
mara touches mara
skin names reveal

her eyes behind sunglasses
his eyes secret
under red band
in the shade they sit

no words are spoken
his eyes secret
her eyes behind sunglasses
in the shade they sit

no words are spoken
Kami sits nearby
not knowing who is in
charge of the flirting

TRUE LOVE

"Let's get married"
she laughed as she
stabbed him in the shoulder
'Sure thing' he laughed
as they walked to the hospital
a half-worn sock
stuffed in the knife hole

the doctor cast quick
glances over his glasses
as he cleaned and
stitched the wound
with disbelief

as they walk down
to their river tree
he picked up a log
hitting it across her back
laughing she grabbed it
wrestling it away
swinging it with all her might
snapping his forearm

back at the hospital
the doctor peers
over his glasses
to stare at a love
that runs deeper
than any wound

BLACK

1.
My father is a unicorn
The mythical beast
Hidden behind clouds
Of gossip.

My mother grasps curtains
Shreds them with anxiety
Plaits ribbons
In an empty church.

My nana opens windows
Weaving songs
And gently tells
Real myths.

2.
My father thinks I am not his

My mother thinks she knows me

My nana thinks I am her heart

But I am none of these

I am white
I am grey
I am black.

YABUN

I hear you as you sit
in silence your eyes search the Dreamtime
crammed in a modern world
Ah!
There are the tjitji of the Dreamtime
maru legs beat drum mara on thighs dance
language voice and laughter
Ah!
There are the kami tjuta of the Dreamtime
quiet under wind whisper shade trees
kuru never rest alert for dangers
ready to fight protect and die
Ah!
Ngunytju tjuta and mama tjuta of the Dreamtime
smile in kuru beautiful people
share soul inma beyond the cultures
another iti of the Dreamtime will be born soon
Ah!
Wati tjuta sit silent
unmoving become rock face and sacred tree
the gibar magic man one with munda
Ah!
I see you on the horizon
in silence you search the Dreamtime
your kuru meet mine in silence
you reveal your presence when you
Smile!

ANANGU LOVE POEMS

1.
I will show you a field of Zebra Finch Dreaming
in the shadow of the stony hill ochre

when the blanket of language hums
and kinship campfires flavour windswept hair

little girls stack single twigs on embers
under Grandfathers skin of painted love

the dance of emu feathers will sweep
the red earth with your smile

do not look at me in daylight
that gift comes in the night

tomorrow I will show Mother
your marriage proposal in my smile

2.
in the cave she rolls *the* big rock for table
for *the* desert wildflowers they pick for one another

she carries many coolamons filled with river sand
to soften the hard rock floor

she makes shelf from braided saplings to hold
all the feathers given by the message birds

while he sleeps she polishes his weapons
with goanna and emu fat till they glisten in fire light

he tells the story of the notches on his spear
the story of the maps on his woomera

their *eyes* fill with spot fires lit on his return
the other women laugh 'get over yourself'

they laugh "he's not that good"
she smiles she knows him in the night

3.
there is love in the wind by the singing rock
down the river by the ancient tree

love in *kangaroo goanna* and *emu*
love when spirits speak no human voice

at the sacred sites eyes unblemished
watch wedge tail eagle soar over hidden water

find the love

TJAMU

Don't cut yr foot on the spinifex grass Grandfather
Your eyes are growing weary
Yet your footprint still strong
Old landscapes cannot fade in yr memory life

Don't hit yr head on the tree branch Grandfather
Your eyes are growing weary
Yet you still stand tall
The Kangaroo Men still visit at night

Don't wait all day at the waterhole Grandfather
Your eyes are growing weary
Yet the path has not ended
The murmur of blessed waters still flows in your veins

Don't cry by the campfire Grandfather
Your eyes are growing weary
Yet the smoke still caresses you
There are no evil Spirits here only love

Don't stay all day in the shade Grandfather
Your eyes are growing weary
Yet sunshine still glows in your skin
The warmth of the humpy fires lives in yr breath

Don't fret about the family Grandfather
Your eyes are weary
Soon to close in peacefulness
After I honour my grieving rituals your eyes will shine in me

WALLAROO

White and wispy beards flap in the sky
Majestic as the storm front approaches
I stare up at the wall of faces
Wise men, Unaipon, Handsome men
Men with anguish I see
Animals that accompany them
Wild boar with razor tusks
A panther cat, buffalo and monkey.

A symphony of colour storms behind
Amber and charcoal and fog floats
Rapid toward me I see old Indians
And other men wrapped in furs, wrinkled
Rippled cloud faces legacies of lifetimes
Battered by the elements, and Life.

I see family who have passed away
And family patriarchs I never met
I see a corpse. Slowly another
Shape emerges – an eagle
So large and so old
So frail yet so strong.
I can see into his cloud skin
This totem being – the oldest
Wedge tail eagle in the world.

The string of men, their anger
and anguish attached are resting on the eagles wing.
The wings stretched far. Determined as

he carries the storm of men on his feathers
Determined to reach the city quickly
Passes overhead.

Behind the rolling drum of thunder
And amber pastel pale floats kindness
Women of song, women of tremendous beauty
Soft and happy supporting their men.
"Let them rage" the women told me
"Because they have been wronged."

They whispered wind words in Kaurna
And Kokatha, in Narrunga and Ngarandjeri.
"Let them rage" the women told me
Through where wrong began when
The grand parents were kicked off the Land
given housing trust and heroin
and then kicked out of there
kicked out of the Square. "Let them rage"
they whisper as the women float past.

Some smile singing in harmonies
Some lay smiling upon white furs
And satin clouds – the feel of luxury
I cannot describe but their smiles above me do

The wind strengthened each heart beat
I saw white streamers as the wind
From under the eagle's wings moved
Across the water. White tips of icing
Upon emerald green and royal navy blue.

Dust and sand blew into my eyes.
Closing them I breathe. I had waited
For that breath for weeks, perhaps months.
I turn to the direction of the city.

I see dust gather where ocean water ends
Dust ghosts climb onto the Land
With huge steps and marching arms
Quickly vanish towards the city

The rain arrives with drums of thunder
On the stage around me wind blasts
My skin and my Soul

I sit at the window
watch the rain
watch the wind
I wonder about the men.
I think of my son.

Lightning flashes instantly
Horizontally a cheeky smile
Across the sky

NOTES

P.9, 'Kami': *kami* – grandmother.

P.10, 'Grade One Primary': 'coon', 'boong', 'abo' are insulting racist terms in Australian English used to refer to Aboriginal people.

P.14, 'Mai': *Mai* – bush food.

P.15, 'Shells: stolen generations' – the term used to identify Aboriginal children who did not grow up with their families because of forced removal or government policy, including adoption.

P.18, 'Tears For Mum': stolen generations – the term used to identify Aboriginal children who did not grow up with their families because of forced removal or government policy, including forced adoption.

P.19, 'Love Dreaming': Haasts Bluff is a small settlement of Luritja and Pintubi people in central Australia.

P.20, 'First time': *munda* – red earth.

P.22, 'Kumana': *kumana* – a term of bereavement given after a family member has died, as it is cultural protocol to not mention their name.

P.23, '2 Pelicans': Daisy Bates was an Irish anthropologist, journalist and welfare worker who lived among the Aboriginal people along the Indian Pacific railway line in Australia for 35 years, including 16 years at Ooldea where my mother was born. *Amoonguna* – Aboriginal town outside Alice Springs. *Arrangkwe* – no, nothing (in Arrernte language).

P.28, 'Ribbons': *Anangu* – name of Aboriginal people living in central Australia. Maralinga is the name of a remote north-western region in South Australia, where the British Government tested atomic weapons in the 1950s and 1960s. The land was returned to the Traditional Owners in 1985, following an agreement between the Australian and British governments' efforts were made to clean up the site. Maralinga Anangu people resettled their land in 1995 and named their new community Oak Valley.

P.29, 'Table Manners': Todd Mall is the main shopping strip in Alice Springs.

P.34, 'Town Camp': *Town camp* is the term given to clusters of Aboriginal housing on the outskirts of Alice Springs and other major remote towns.

P.40, 'Ngankari': *Ngankari* – Anangu traditional healer. The Seven Sisters Dreaming story is represented in the sky by the Pleiades cluster.

P.41, 'Sunrise': *Pipalyatjara* – a remote town in the Anangu Pitjantjatjara Yankunytjatjara Lands of north west South Australia; *inma* – traditional dance and song ceremony; *Kupa Piti Kungka Tjuta* – the group of Grandmothers who lived in Coober Pedy, that fought and won the fight to stop the Federal government's plan to build a nuclear waste dump in the traditional Yankunytjatjara and Antikarinya Lands in South Australia; *munda* – the earth. Frank Yamma is a Pitjantjatjara singer songwriter of international acclaim.

P.44, 'A Parable': *rifela* – rifles; *rama rama* – crazy, mad.

P.45, 'Intervention Payback': *wali* – house; *tjamu* – grandfather; CDEP – Community Development Empolyment Projects; *ninti* – clever; *malu* – kangaroo; *kungkas* – women.

P.50, 'Palya': *palya* – hello how are you?; *mara* – hand.

P.53, 'Yabun': Yabun is the name of an Indigenous festival on January 26, the Australia Day public holiday, that recognises the arrival of Captain Cook at Botany Bay. *tjitji* – children; *maru* – black; *kami tjuta* – many grandmothers; *kuru* – eyes; *ngunytju tjuta* – many wives; *mama tjuta* – many husbands; *wati tjuta* – many men; *iti* – baby; *gibar* – a magic man from Queensland.

P.54, 'Anangu Love Poems': *coolamons* – traditional Aboriginal dish made of wood; *woomera* – traditional Aboriginal shield made of wood.

P.57, 'Wallaroo': Wallaroo is a beach on the Yorke Peninsula of South Australia.

Lightning Source UK Ltd.
Milton Keynes UK
UKOW05f1914020317
295772UK00022B/1171/P

9 781922 181725